PIANO • VOCAL • GUITAR

ELTON JOHN
ROCKET MAN • NUMBER ONES

CONTENTS

- 2 Goodbye Yellow Brick Road
- 6 Bennie and the Jets
- 10 Daniel
- 15 Crocodile Rock
- 20 Lucy in the Sky with Diamonds
- 24 Philadelphia Freedom
- 34 Island Girl
- 29 Don't Go Breaking My Heart
- 40 Sorry Seems to Be the Hardest Word
- 44 Sacrifice
- 48 Don't Let the Sun Go Down on Me
- 62 Can You Feel the Love Tonight
- 66 Your Song
- 72 Tiny Dancer
- 78 Rocket Man (I Think It's Gonna Be a Long Long Time)
- 55 Candle in the Wind
- 84 Saturday Night's Alright (For Fighting)

ISBN-13: 978-1-4234-3086-5
ISBN-10: 1-4234-3086-7

HAL•LEONARD®
CORPORATION
7777 W. BLUEMOUND RD. P.O. BOX 13819 MILWAUKEE, WI 53213

Visit Hal Leonard Online at
www.halleonard.com

GOODBYE YELLOW BRICK ROAD

Words and Music by ELTON JOHN
and BERNIE TAUPIN

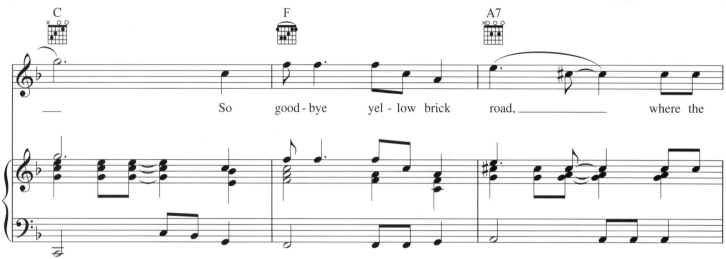

So good-bye yel-low brick road, _____ where the

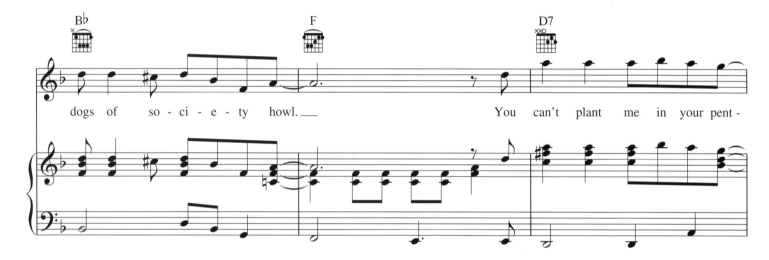

dogs of so-ci-e-ty howl. ___ You can't plant me in your pent-

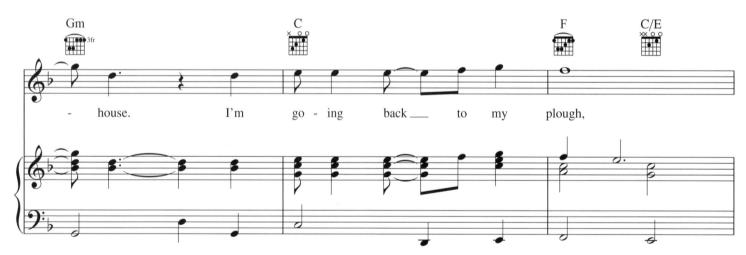

- house. I'm go-ing back ___ to my plough,

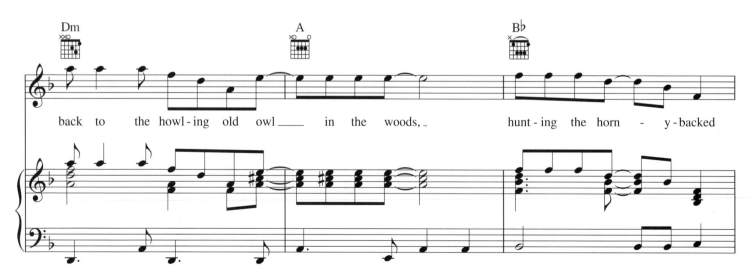

back to the howl-ing old owl ___ in the woods, _ hunt-ing the horn-y-backed

BENNIE AND THE JETS

Words and Music by ELTON JOHN
and BERNIE TAUPIN

Slowly, deliberately

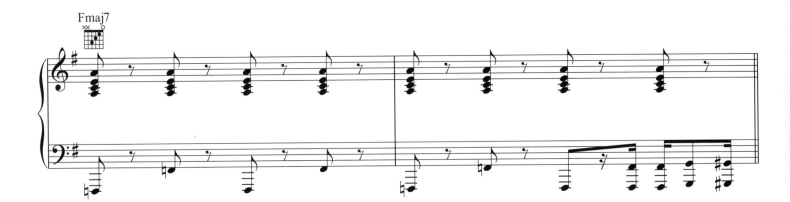

Hey, kids, __ shake it loose to-geth - er. The spot - light's hit - ting some-thing that's been known to change the weath - er.
Hey, kids, __ plug __ in - to the faith-less. May - be they're __ blind - ed, __ but Ben-nie makes them age - less.
Solo ad lib.

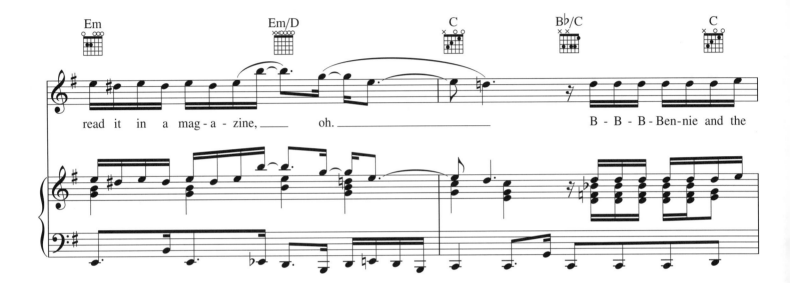

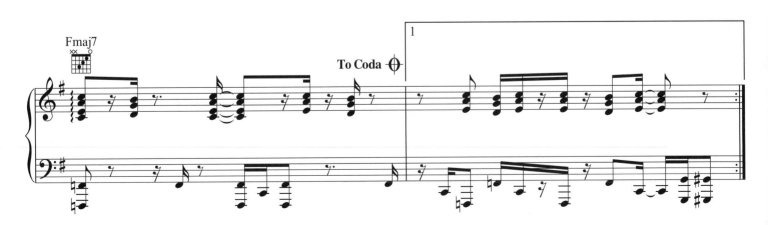

DANIEL

Words and Music by ELTON JOHN
and BERNIE TAUPIN

Moderately fast

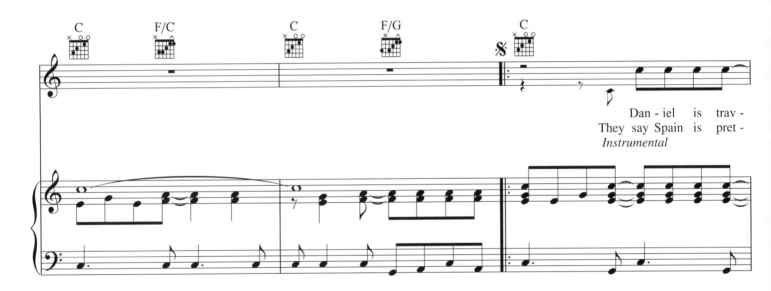

Dan - iel is trav -
They say Spain is pret -
Instrumental

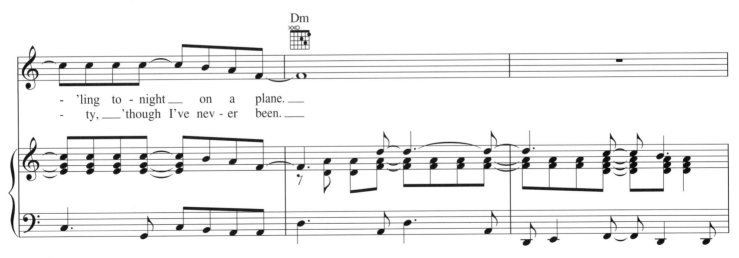

- 'ling to - night ___ on a plane. ___
- ty, ___ 'though I've nev - er been. ___

I can see the red tail-lights head-ing for Spain.
Well, Dan-iel says it's the best place he's ev - er seen.

Oh, and I can see Dan - iel wav - ing good-bye.
Oh, and he should know; he's been there e - nough.

God, it looks like Dan - iel.
Lord, I miss Dan - iel.

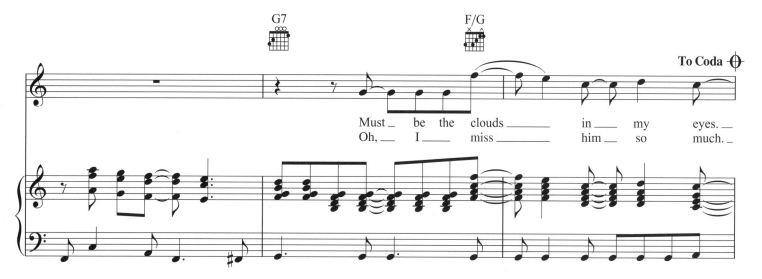

To Coda

Must be the clouds in my eyes.
Oh, I miss him so much.

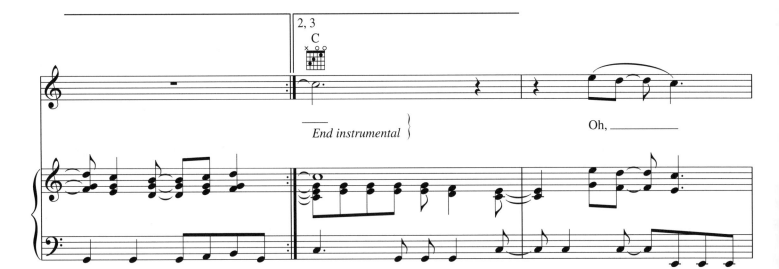

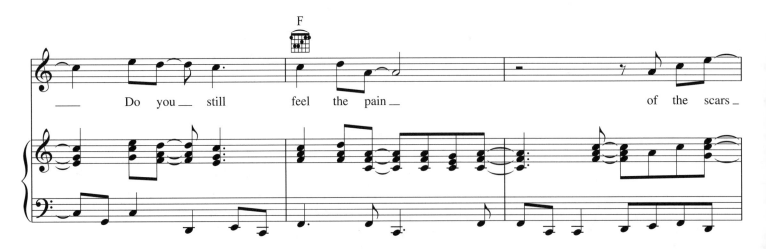

that ___ won't heal? ___ Your eyes ___ have ___ died, _____ but

you see more ___ than ___ I. _____ Dan - iel, you're a

star ___ in the face ___ of the sky. _____

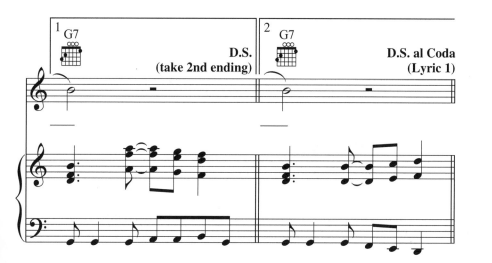

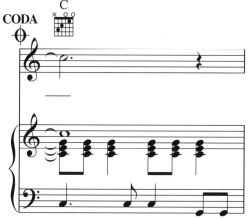

Oh God, _____ it looks like Dan - iel.

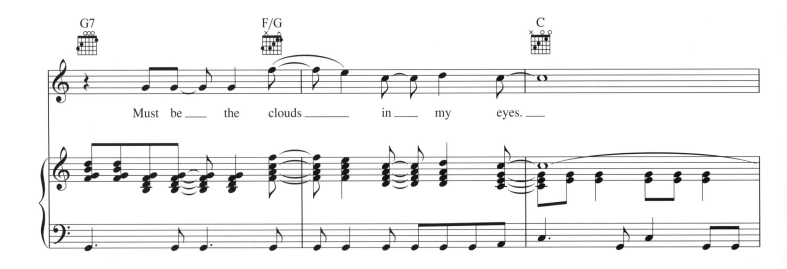

Must be _____ the clouds _____ in _____ my _____ eyes. _____

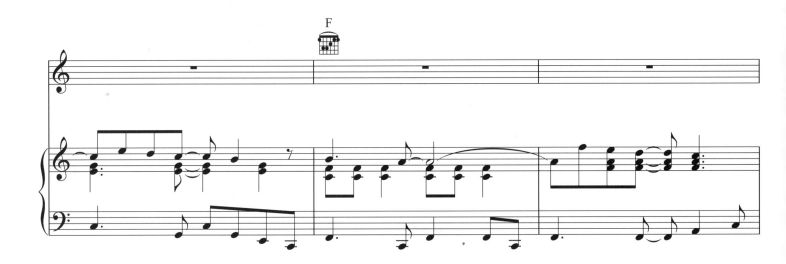

CROCODILE ROCK

Words and Music by ELTON JOHN
and BERNIE TAUPIN

Light-hearted Rock

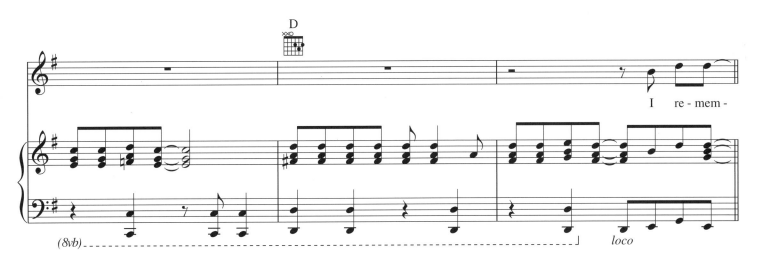

I re-mem-

(1., 3.) -ber when rock was young. _____ Me and Su - sie had so much fun _____

_____ went by _____ and rock just died. _ Su - sie went and left me for some

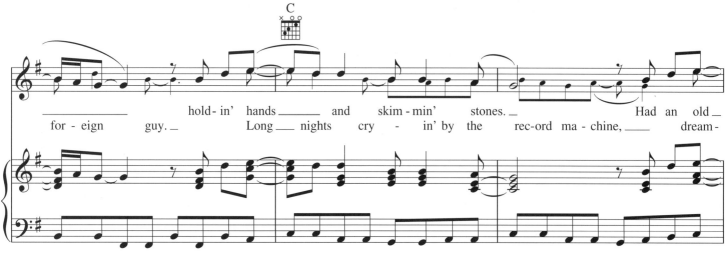

hold-in' hands _____ and skim-min' stones. __ Had an old __
for-eign guy. __ Long ___ nights cry - in' by the rec-ord ma-chine, ___ dream-

___ gold Chev-y and a place of my own. __ But the big - gest kick I ev - er got __
- in' of my Chev-y and my old __ blue jeans. __ But they'll nev - er kill the thrills we've got __

_____ was do-ing a thing called the croc-o-dile rock. _____ While the oth -
_____ burn - ing up to the croc-o-dile rock. _____ Learn-ing fast __

- er kids were rock-ing 'round the clock, __ we were hop - pin' and bop - pin' to the
_____ as the weeks went __ past, __ we real - ly thought __ the croc - o - dile __

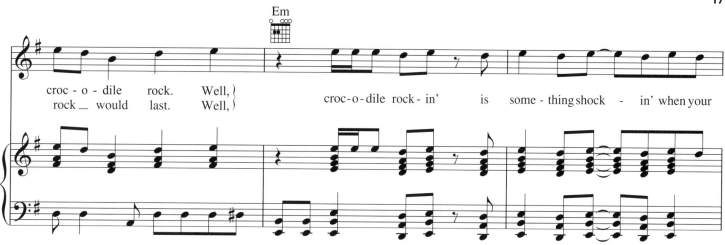

croc - o - dile rock. Well,
rock _ would last. Well,

croc-o-dile rock-in' is some-thing shock - in' when your

feet just can't keep still. _

I nev - er knew me a

bet - ter time _ and I guess _ I nev - er _ will. _

Oh, _

_____ Lawd - y, ma - ma, those Fri - day nights _ when Su - sie wore _ her

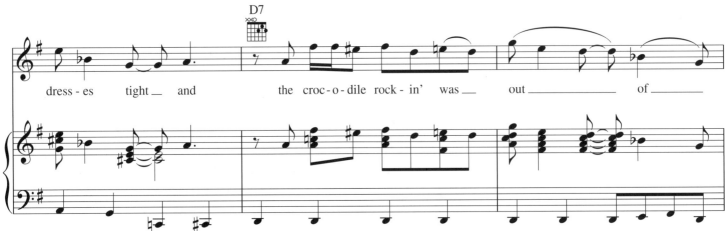

dress - es tight __ and the croc-o-dile rock - in' was __ out _____ of __

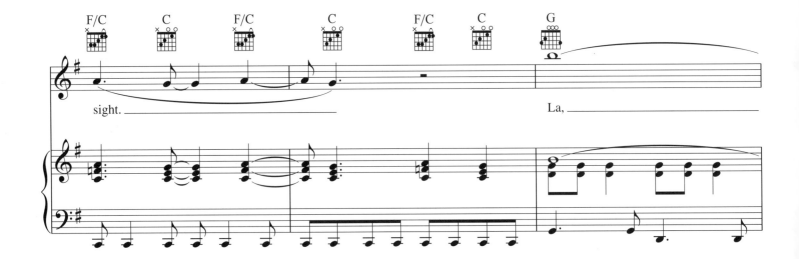

sight. _____ La, _____

__ la la la la la, _____ la la la la

la, _____ la la la la la.

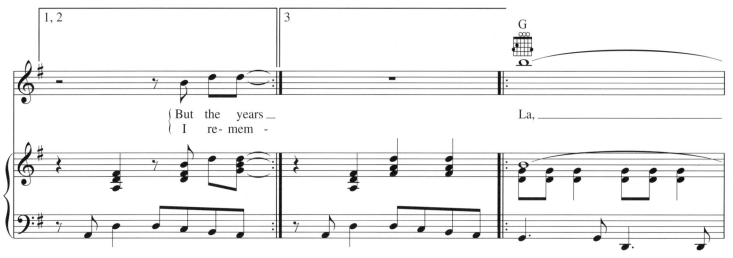

But the years
I re- mem -
La,

la la la la la, la la la la

Repeat and Fade

la, la la la la la.

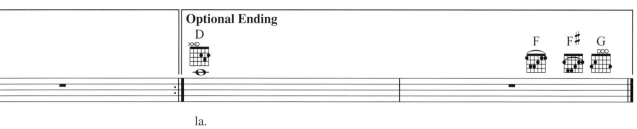

Optional Ending

la.

LUCY IN THE SKY WITH DIAMONDS

Words and Music by JOHN LENNON
and PAUL McCARTNEY

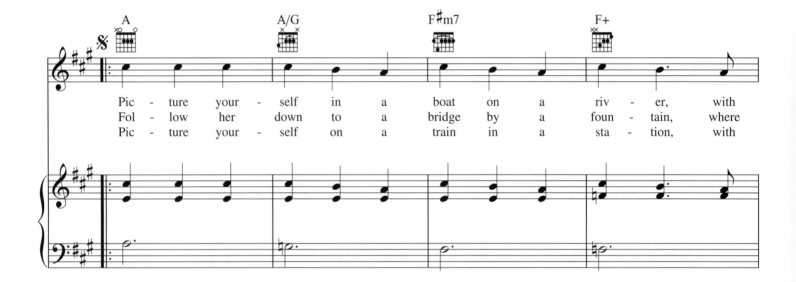

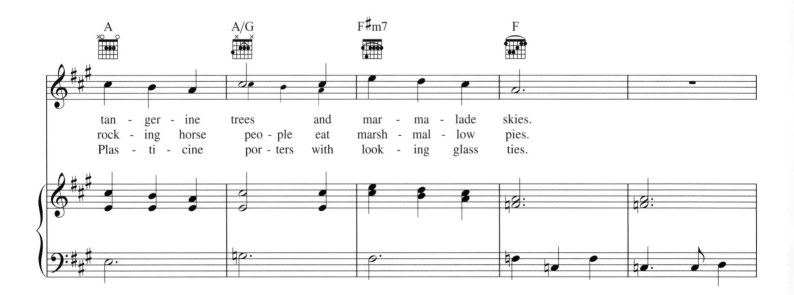

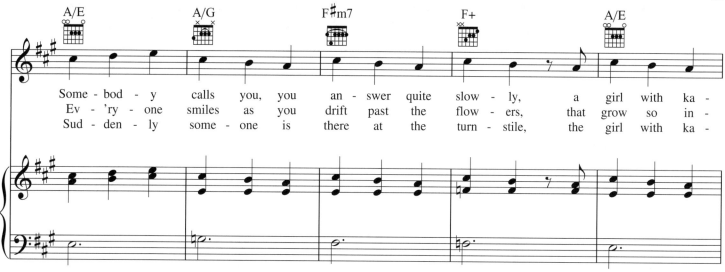

Some-bod - y calls you, you an - swer quite slow - ly, a girl with ka -
Ev - 'ry - one smiles as you drift past the flow - ers, that grow so in -
Sud - den - ly some - one is there at the turn - stile, the girl with ka -

lei - do - scope eyes. _____
cred - i - bly high. _____
lei - do - scope

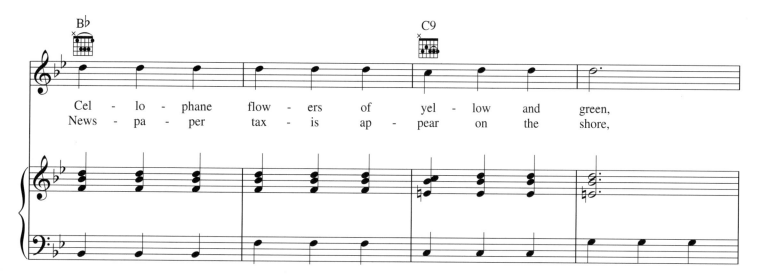

Cel - lo - phane flow - ers of yel - low and green,
News - pa - per tax - is ap - pear on the shore,

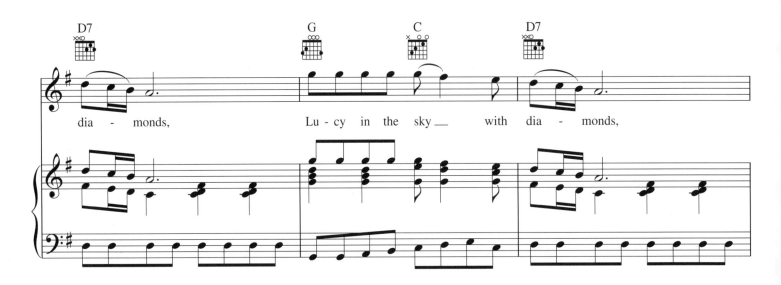

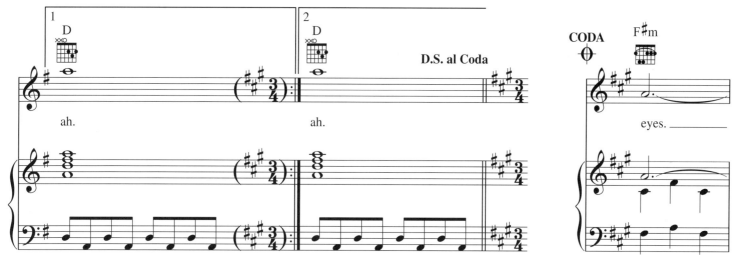

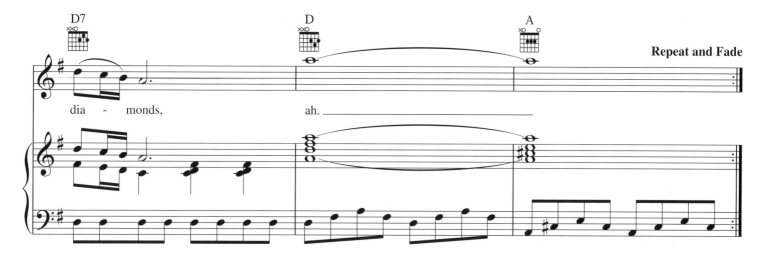

PHILADELPHIA FREEDOM

Words and Music by ELTON JOHN
and BERNIE TAUPIN

With a beat

used to be a roll - ing stone, __ you know. __ If the cause __ was right, __
2. *(See additional lyrics)*

I'd leave _____ to find the an - swer on __ the road. __

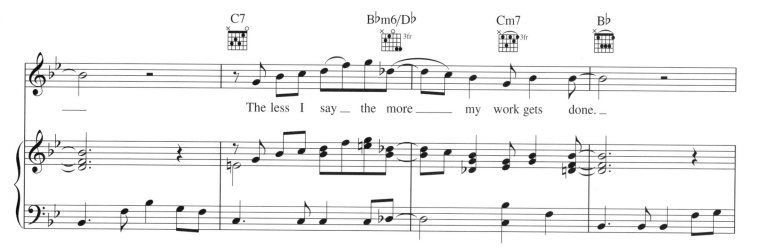

Phil-a-del-phia free-dom took me knee-high to a man.

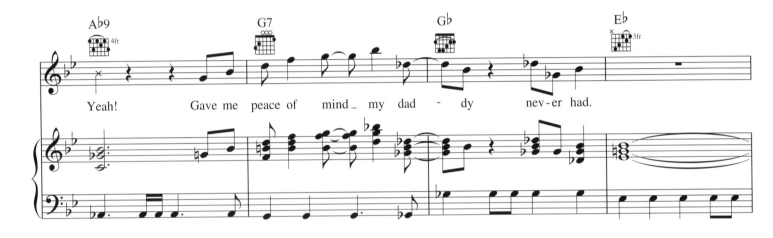

Yeah! Gave me peace of mind_ my dad — dy nev-er had.

Oh, Phil-a-del-phi-a free-dom shine on me._____ I love_

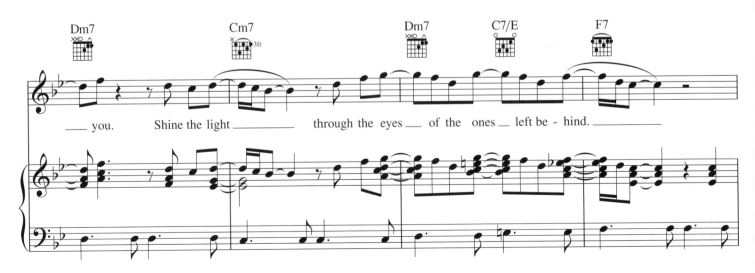

__ you. Shine the light_____ through the eyes__ of the ones__ left be-hind._____

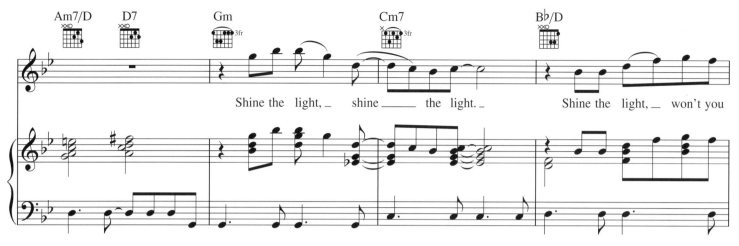

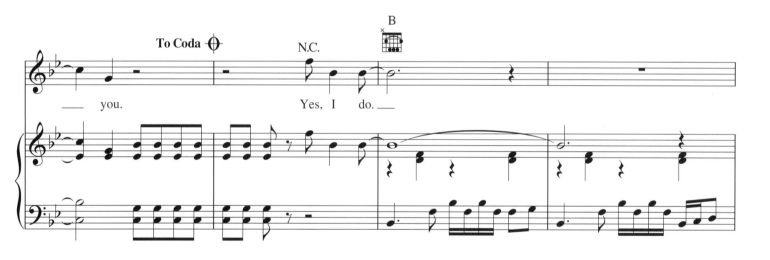

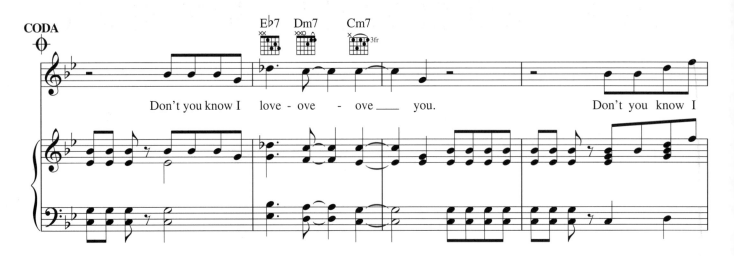

Additional Lyrics

2. If you choose to, you can live your life alone.
   Some people choose the city,
   Some others choose the good old family home.
   I like living easy without family ties,
   'Til the whippoorwill of freedom zapped me
   Right between the eyes.

Chorus

DON'T GO BREAKING MY HEART

Words and Music by CARTE BLANCHE
and ANN ORSON

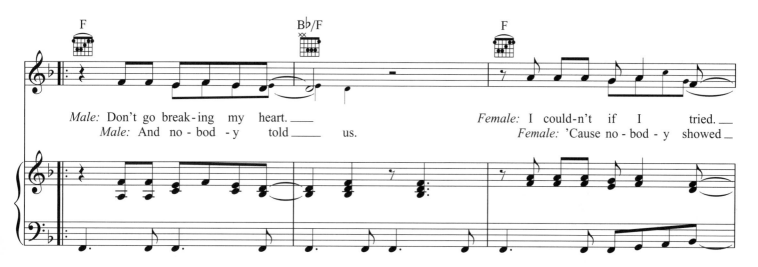

Male: Don't go break-ing my heart. ___
Male: And no-bod-y told ___ us.

Female: I could-n't if I tried. ___
Female: 'Cause no-bod-y showed ___

___ us.

Male: Oh, hon-ey, if I ___ get rest-less...
Male: And, now ___ it's up ___ to us, ___ babe.

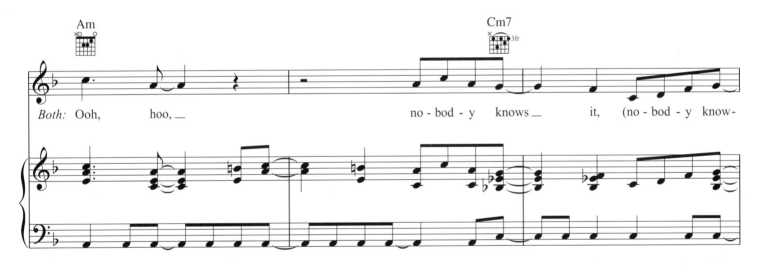

Oh, _____ oh, ____ I gave you my heart. _____

Male: So, don't go break-ing my heart. _____

To Coda ⊕

Female: I won't go break-ing your heart. __

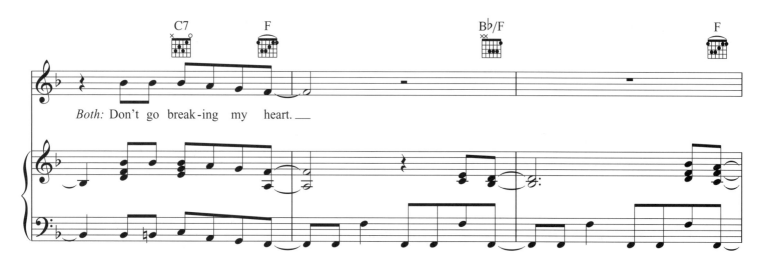

Both: Don't go break-ing my heart. __

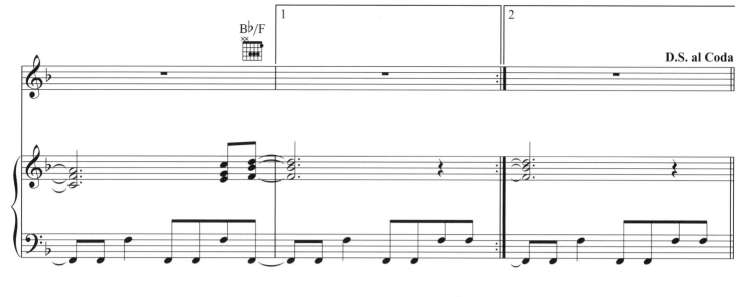

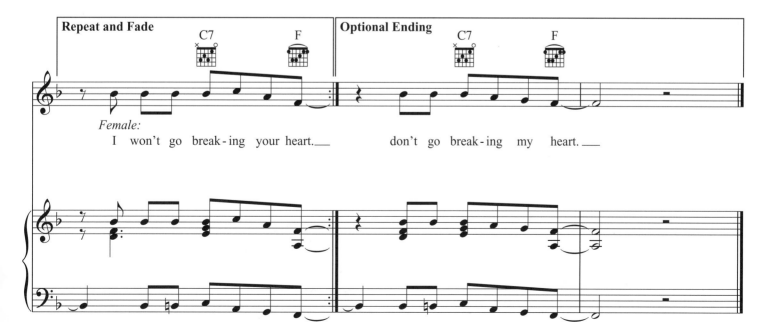

ISLAND GIRL

Words and Music by ELTON JOHN
and BERNIE TAUPIN

Moderately fast

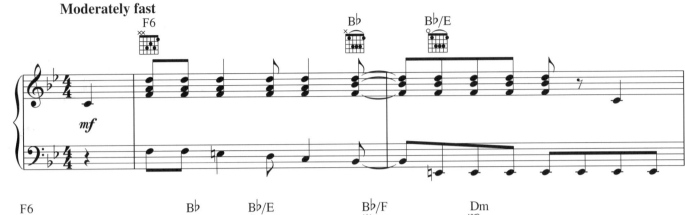

I see your teeth flash, Ja-

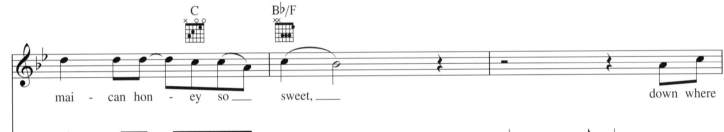

mai - can hon - ey so ___ sweet, ___ down where

Lex - ing - ton ___ cross For - ty - sev - enth Street. ___

Oh, _____ she's a big _____ girl, she's stand-ing six-foot _____ three, _____

_____ turn-ing tricks for the dudes _____ in the

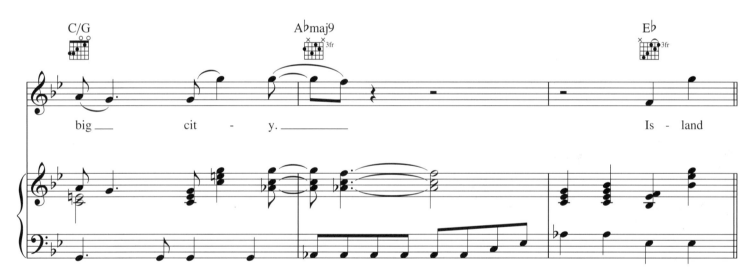

big _____ cit - y. _____ Is - land

girl, what you want - in' wid de white man's world? _____

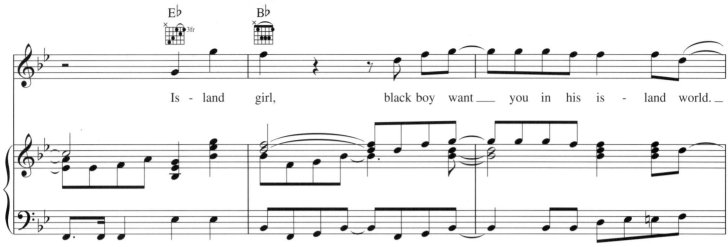

Is - land girl, black boy want__ you in his is - land world.__

_____ He want to take you from de

rack - et boss.__ He want to save you,__ but de cause_____ is lost.__

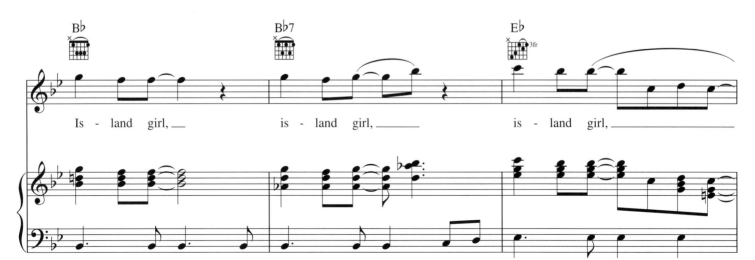

Is - land girl, __ is - land girl, _____ is - land girl, _____

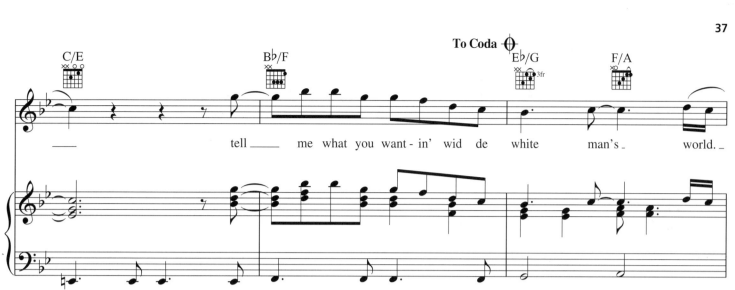

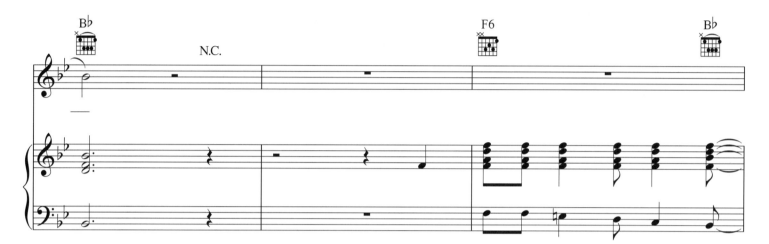

and she wrap ___ her-self a-round you   like a well-worn tire. ___

___ You feel her nail scratch ___ your ___ back ___

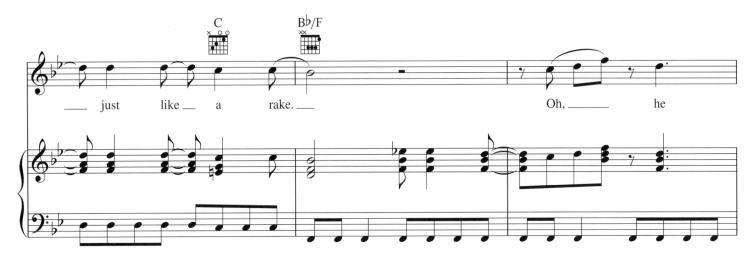

___ just like ___ a rake. ___   Oh, ___ he

one more gone, ___ he one ___ more john ___ who make ___ de mis-take. ___
End instrumental

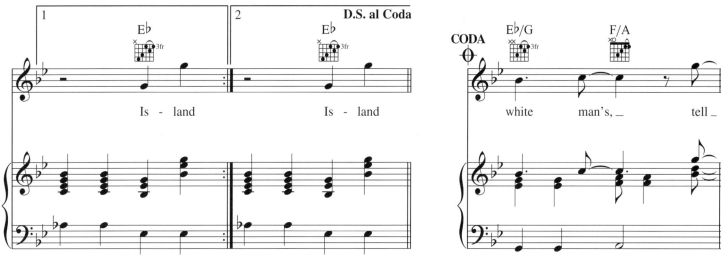

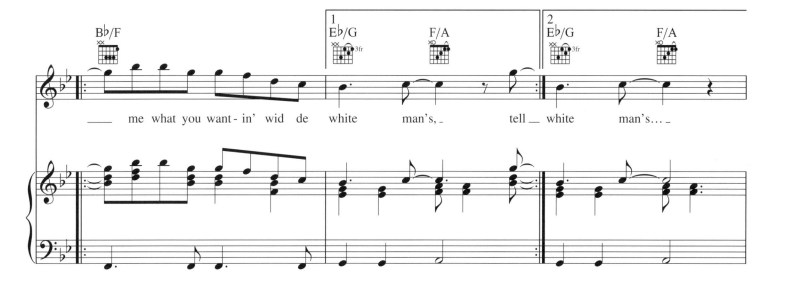

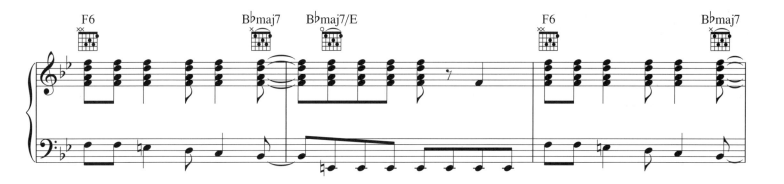

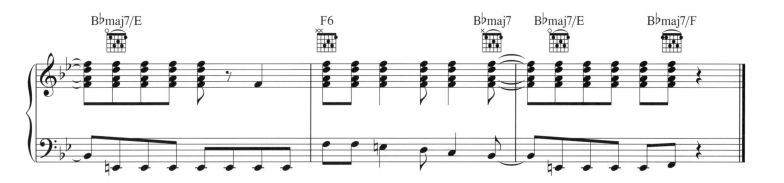

SORRY SEEMS TO BE THE HARDEST WORD

Words and Music by ELTON JOHN
and BERNIE TAUPIN

Slow lament

It's so sad, __ so sad. __ Why can't __ we talk __ it o - ver? __ Oh, it seems to me _____ that
(so sad)

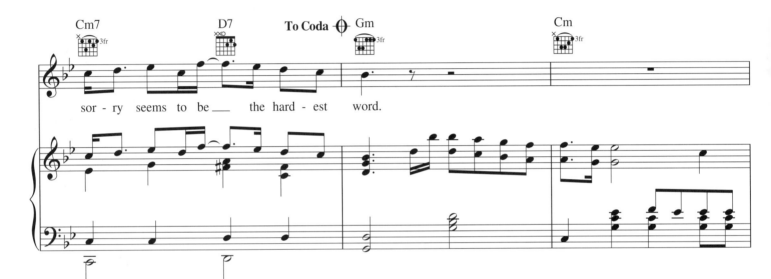

sor - ry seems to be __ the hard - est word.

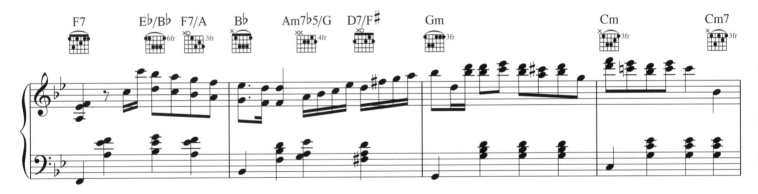

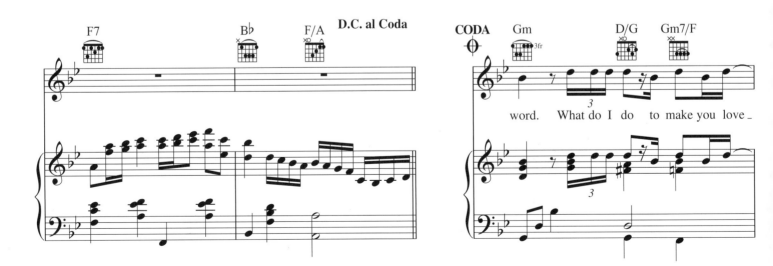

word. What do I do to make you love __

SACRIFICE

Words and Music by ELTON JOHN
and BERNIE TAUPIN

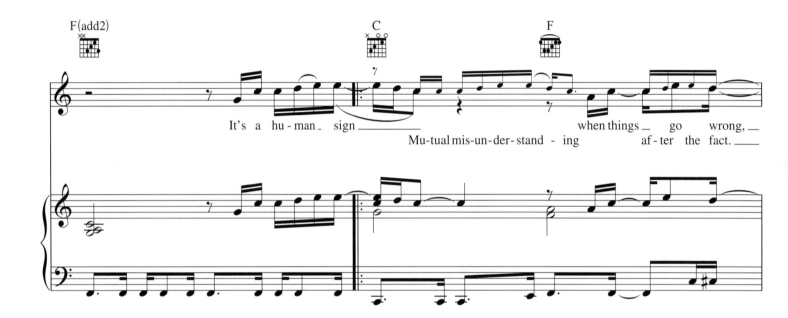

It's a hu-man sign _____ when things _ go wrong,
Mu-tual mis-un-der-stand - ing af-ter the fact. _____

_____ when the scent of her lin - gers _____ and temp - ta-tion's strong.
_____ Sen-si-tiv-i-ty builds _ a pris-on in the fi-nal act. _____

* Recorded a half step higher.

And it's no sac-ri-fice, ___ just a sim-ple ___ word. ___ It's two hearts liv-

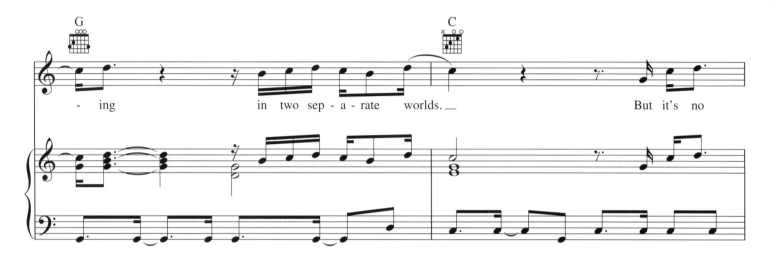

-ing in two sep-a-rate worlds. ___ But it's no

sac-ri-fice, ___ no sac-ri-fice, ___ it's no sac-

ri-fice ___ at ___ all. ___

DON'T LET THE SUN GO DOWN ON ME

Words and Music by ELTON JOHN
and BERNIE TAUPIN

Slow beat

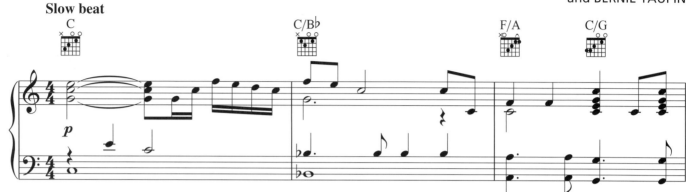

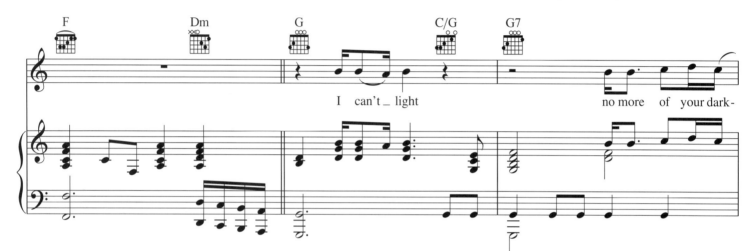

I can't _ light

no more of your dark-

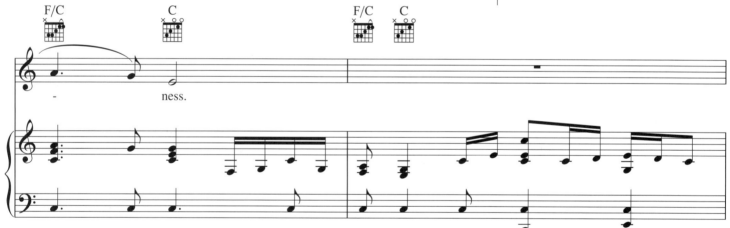

- ness.

All my pic - tures _____ seem to fade _ to black _ and white.

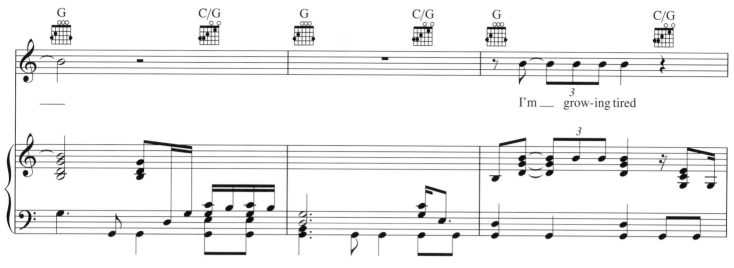

I'm ___ grow-ing tired

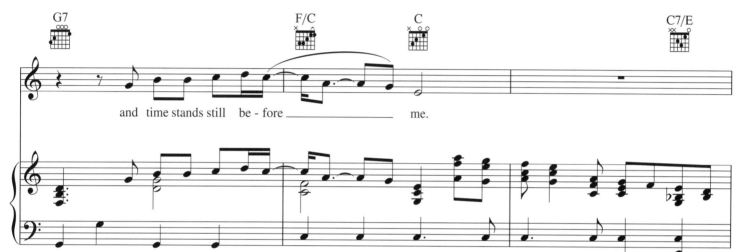

and time stands still be - fore _____ me.

Fro - zen here, ___ on the lad - der of ___ my ___

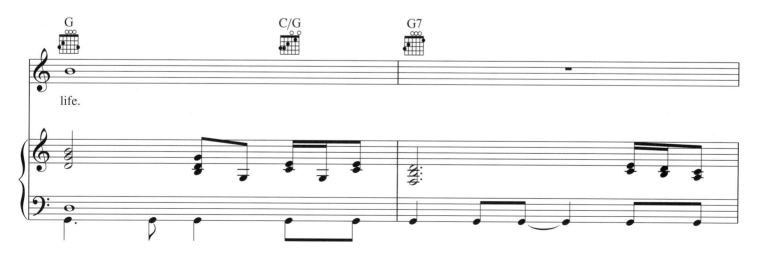

life.

Too late ___ to save my-self from fall - ing.

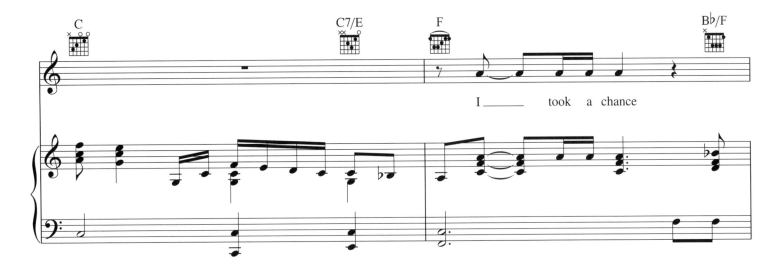

I ___ took a chance

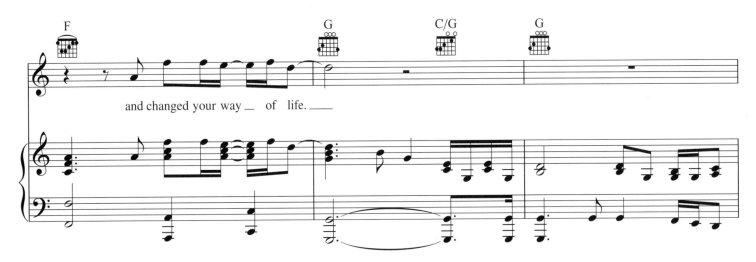

and changed your way ___ of life. ___

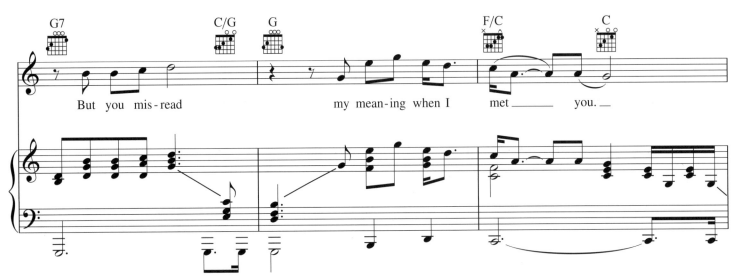

But you mis-read my mean-ing when I met ___ you. ___

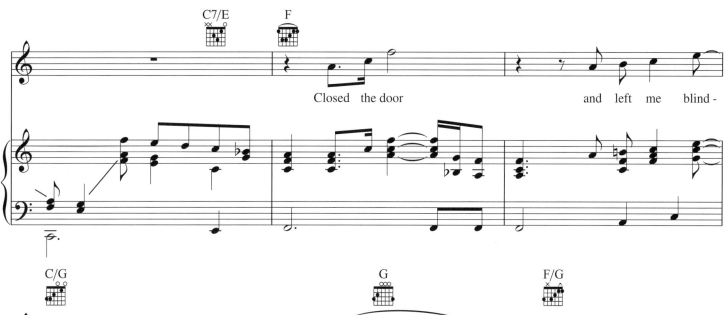

Closed the door and left me blind-

-ed _____ by _____ the light. _____

Don't let the sun _____ go down on me. _____

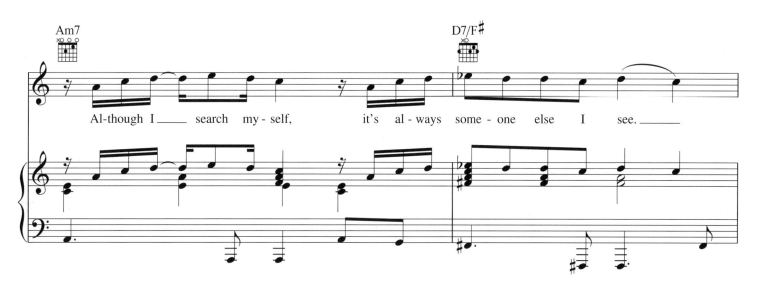

Al-though I _____ search my-self, it's al-ways some-one else I see. _____

I'd just al-low a frag-ment of your life _____ to wan-der free. __

_____ But

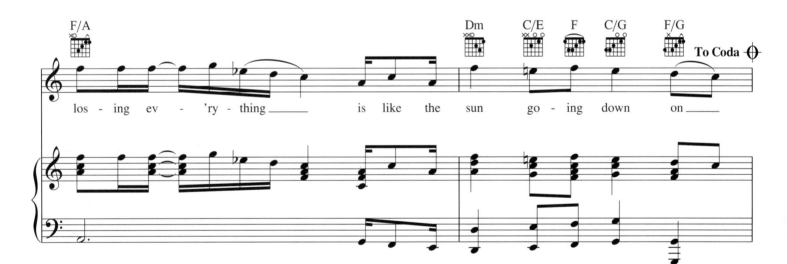

los-ing ev-'ry-thing _____ is like the sun go-ing down on _____

To Coda ⊕

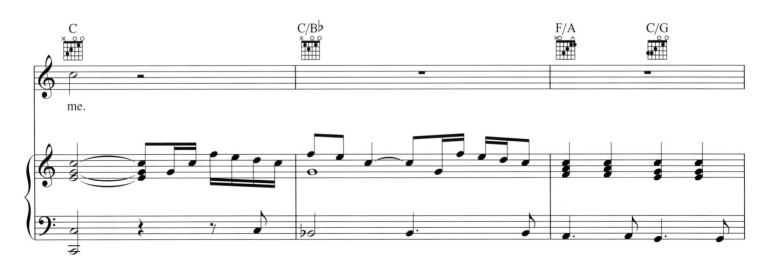

me.

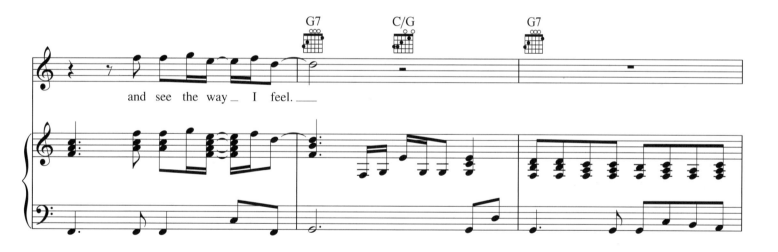

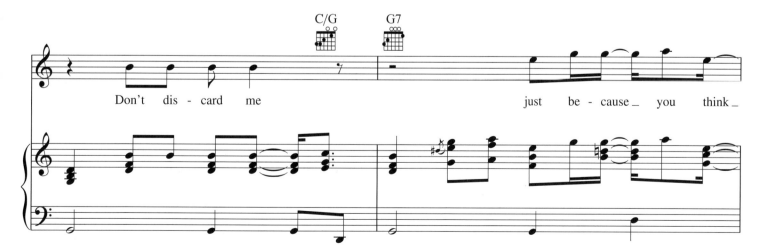

I mean you harm.

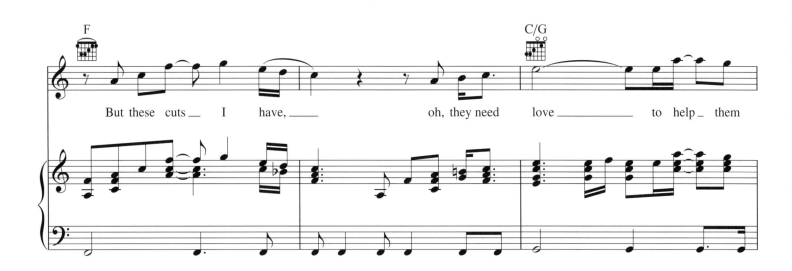

But these cuts I have, oh, they need love to help them

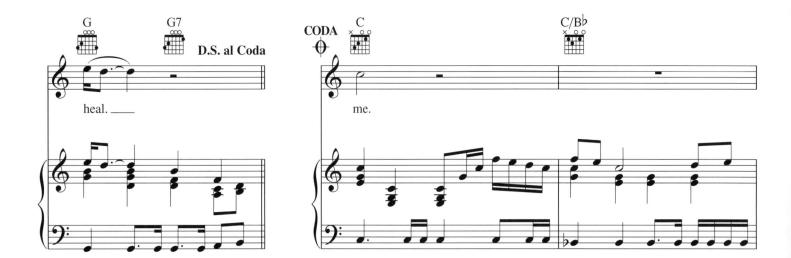

heal. me.

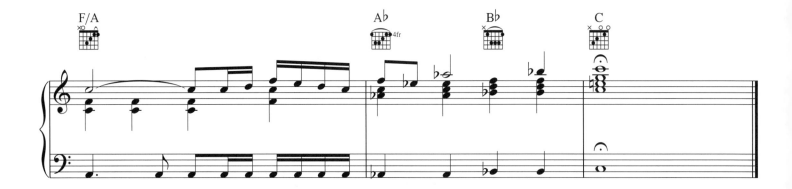

CANDLE IN THE WIND

Words and Music by ELTON JOHN
and BERNIE TAUPIN

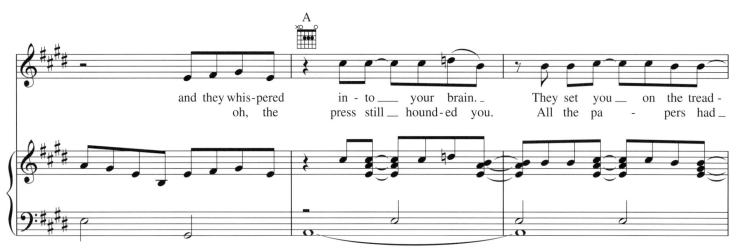

and they whis-pered in-to ___ your brain. ___ They set you ___ on the tread-
oh, the press still ___ hound-ed you. All the pa - pers had ___

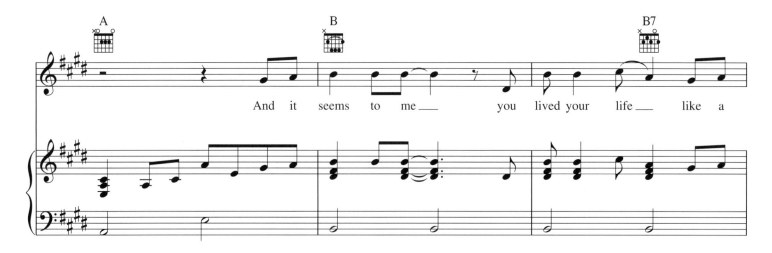

- mill ___ and they made you change ___ your name. ___
___ to ___ say was that Mar - i - lyn was found in the nude.

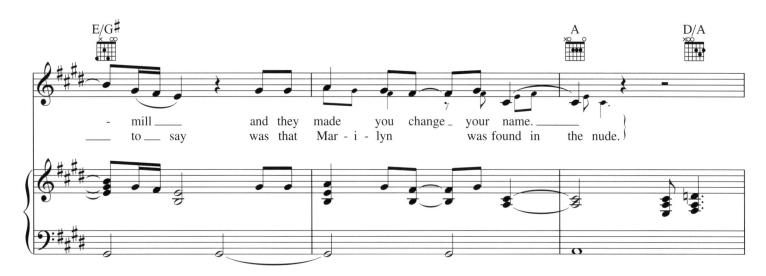

And it seems to me ___ you lived your life ___ like a

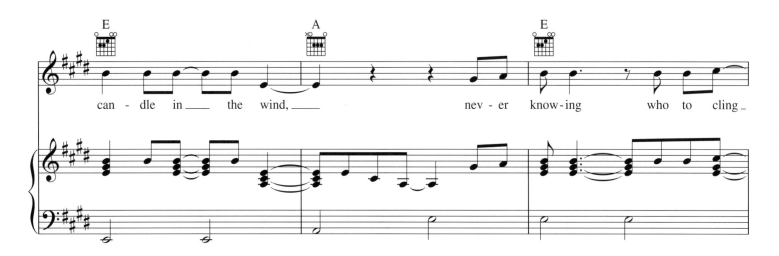

can - dle in ___ the wind, ___ nev - er know-ing who to cling ___

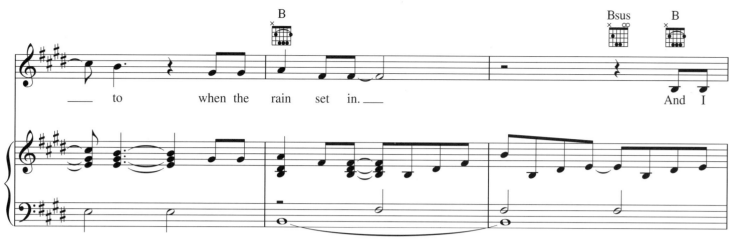

to when the rain set in. ___ And I

would have liked ___ to have known you, but I was just ___ a kid. Your

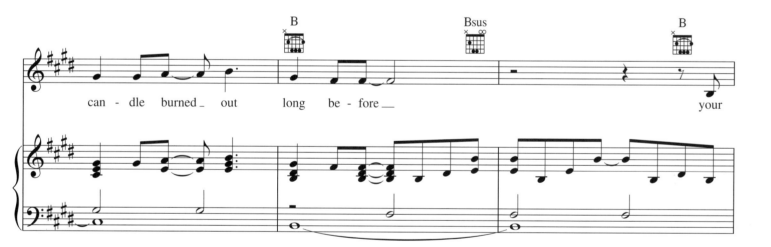

can - dle burned ___ out long be - fore ___ your

leg - end ev - er did. ___

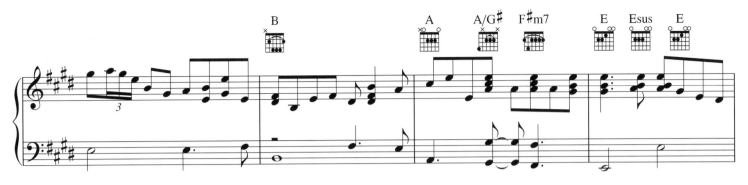

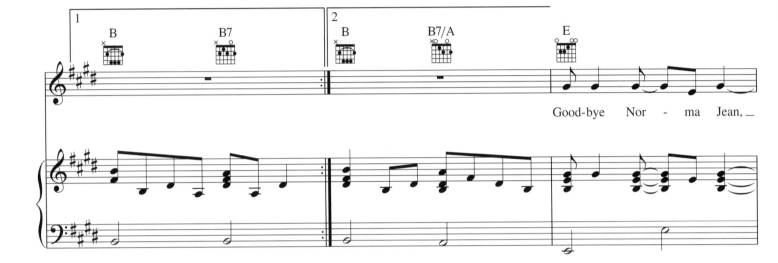

Good-bye Nor - ma Jean, __ though I nev - er knew you __ at all, you had the grace to

hold your-self _____ while those a - round __ you crawled. __

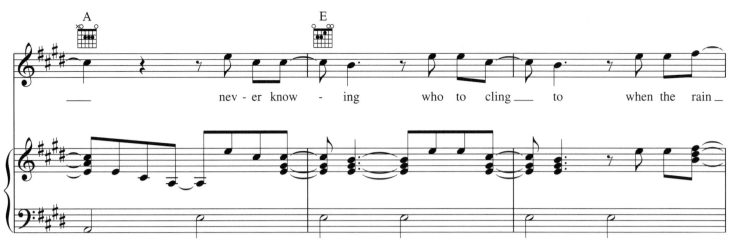

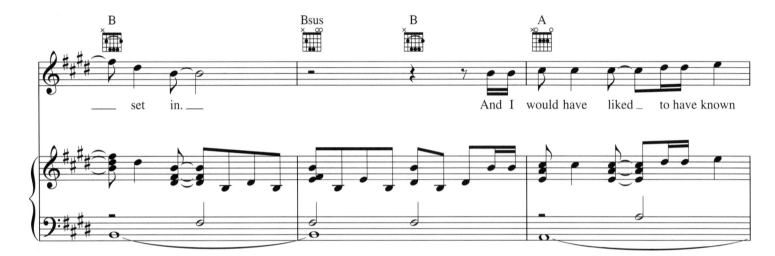

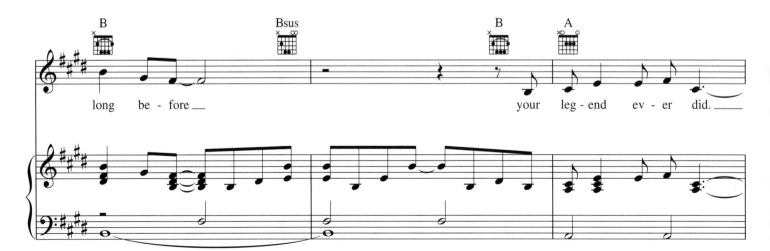

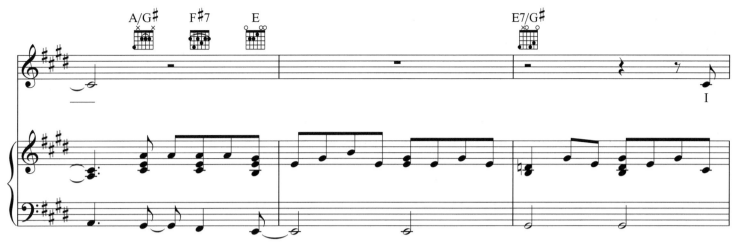

would have liked to have known you, whoa, but I was just a kid.

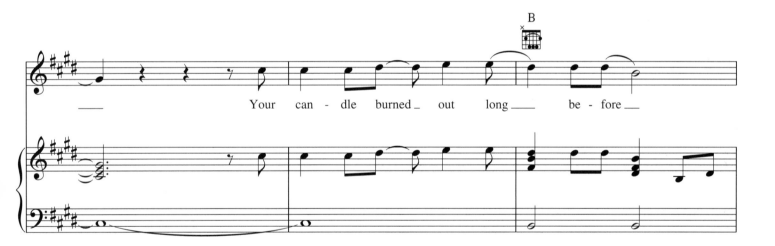

Your can - dle burned out long be - fore

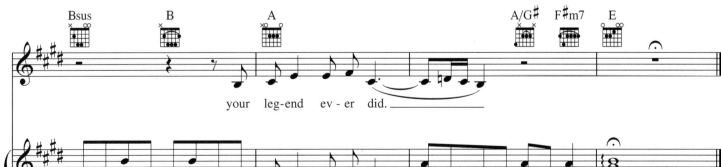

your leg-end ev - er did.

rit.

CAN YOU FEEL THE LOVE TONIGHT

from Walt Disney Pictures' THE LION KING

Music by ELTON JOHN
Lyrics by TIM RICE

and it sees __ me through. __ It's e - nough __ for this rest - less war - rior
to the wild __ out - doors __ when the heart __ of this star - crossed voy - ag - er

just to be __ with you.
beats in time __ with yours.

And can you feel __ the love __

poco cresc.

__ to - night? __ It is where __ we are. __

It's e - nough __ for this

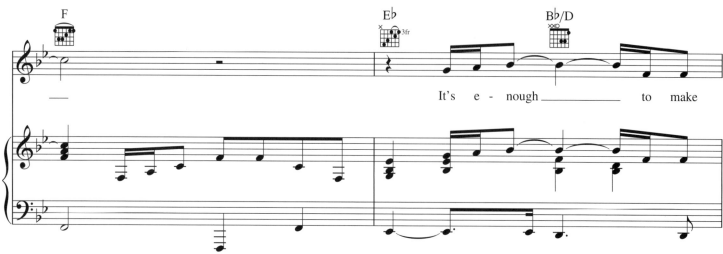

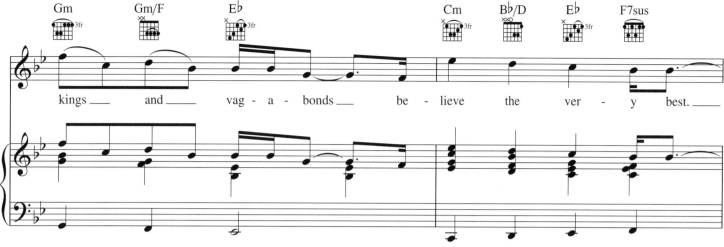

kings ___ and ___ vag - a - bonds ___ be - lieve the ver - y best. ___

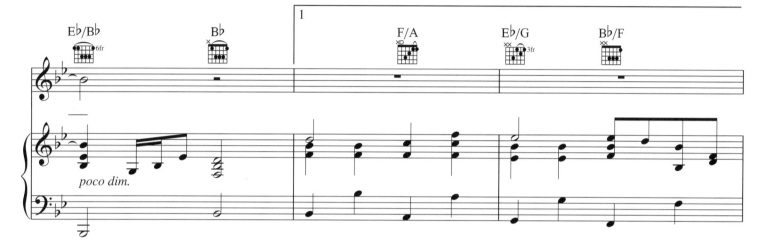

poco dim.

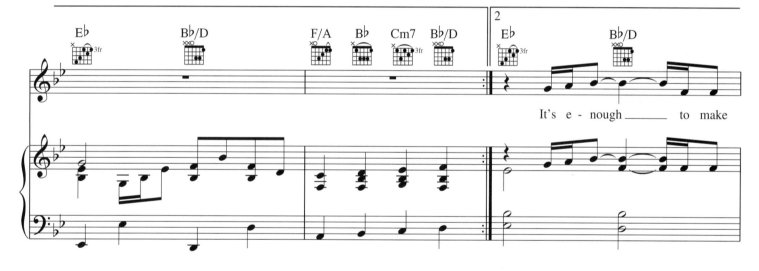

It's e - nough ___ to make

kings _ and _ vag - a - bonds _ be - lieve the ver - y best. ___

molto rit.

YOUR SONG

Words and Music by ELTON JOHN
and BERNIE TAUPIN

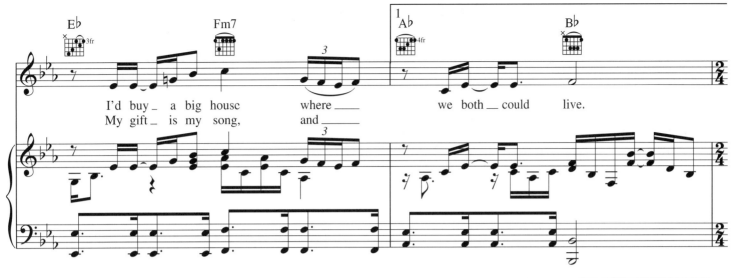

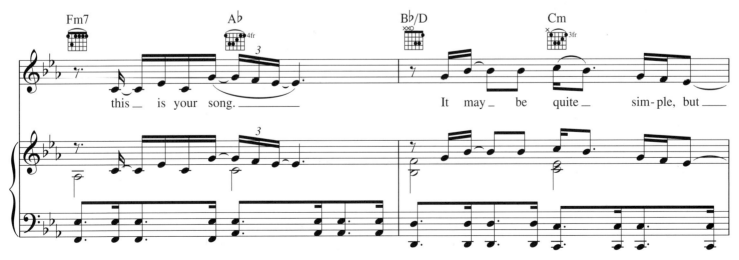

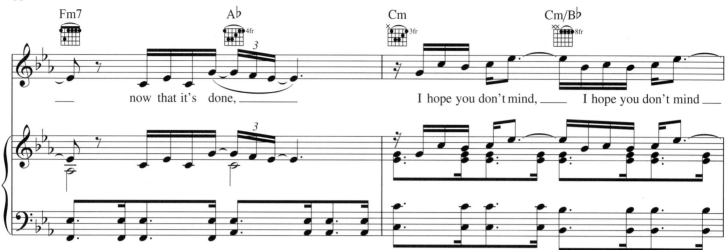

now that it's done, _____ I hope you don't mind, _____ I hope you don't mind ___

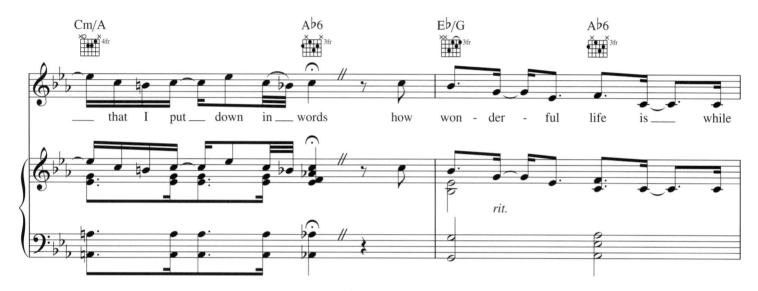

_____ that I put ___ down in ___ words how won - der - ful life is ___ while

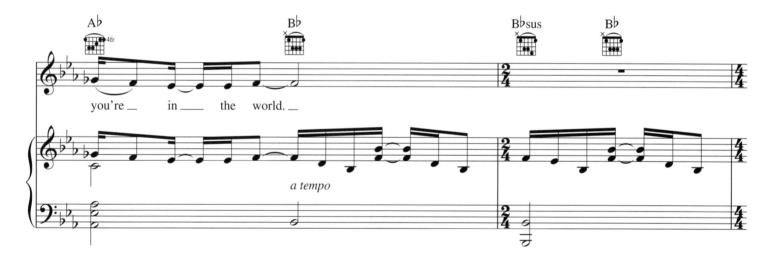

you're ___ in ___ the world. ___

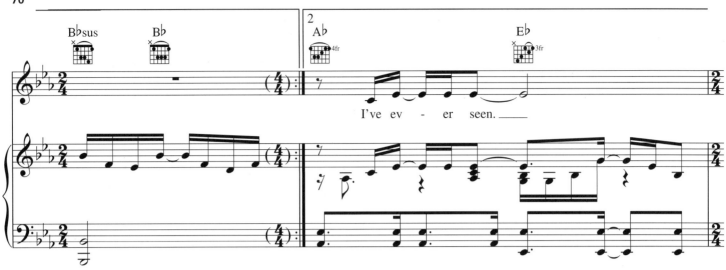

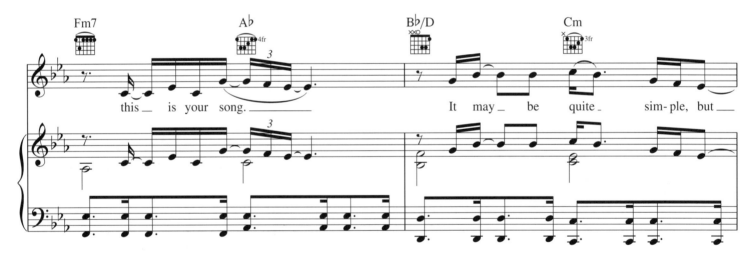

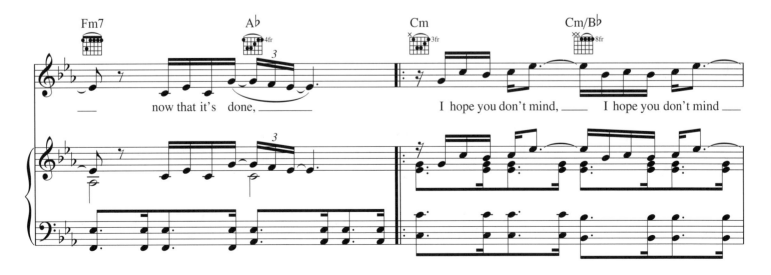

that I put down in words how won-der-ful life is while

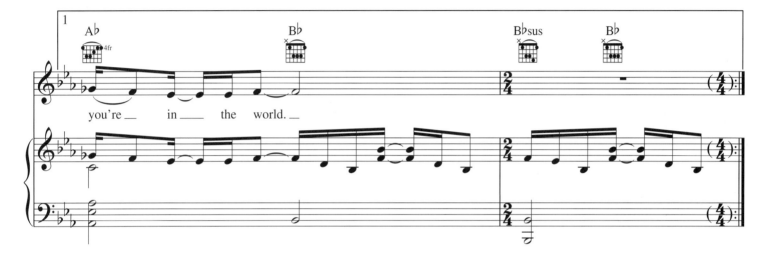

you're in the world.

you're in the world.

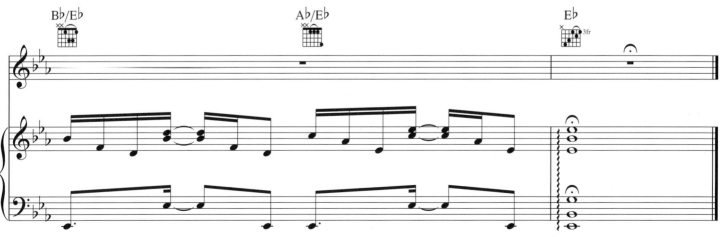

TINY DANCER

Words and Music by ELTON JOHN
and BERNIE TAUPIN

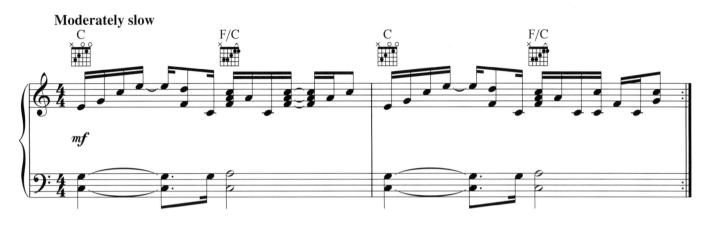

(1., 3.) Blue - jean ba - by. ___ L. ___ A. la - dy. ___
(2.) Je - sus freaks ___ out in ___ the ___ street ___

Seam - stress for ___ the band. ___
hand - ing tick - ets out ___ for God. ___

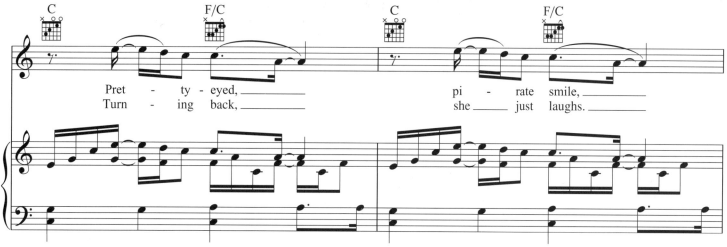

Pret - ty - eyed, _____ pi - rate smile, _____
Turn - ing back, _____ she _____ just laughs. _____

you'll mar-ry a mu - sic man. _____
The boul-e-vard is not that bad. _____

Bal - le - ri - na.
Pia - no _____ man, _____ You must _____ have seen _____ her
he makes _____ his stand _____

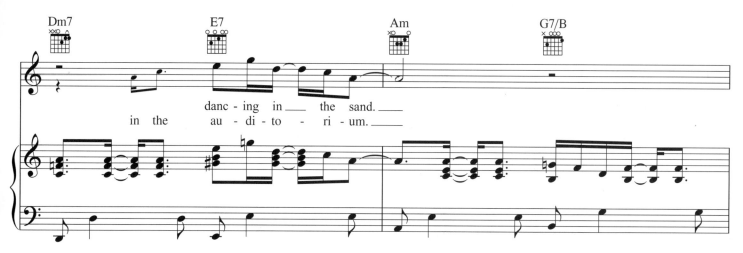

danc - ing in _____ the sand. _____
in the au - di - to - ri - um. _____

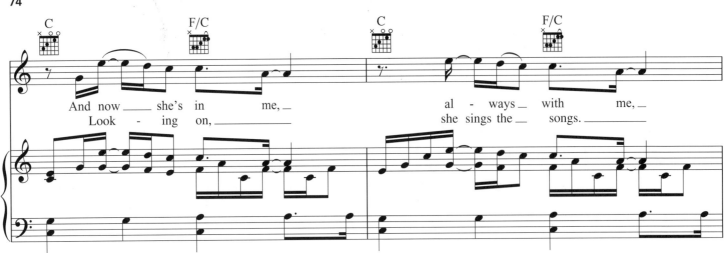

And now _____ she's in me, _ al - ways _ with me, _
Look - ing on, _____

she sings the _ songs. _____

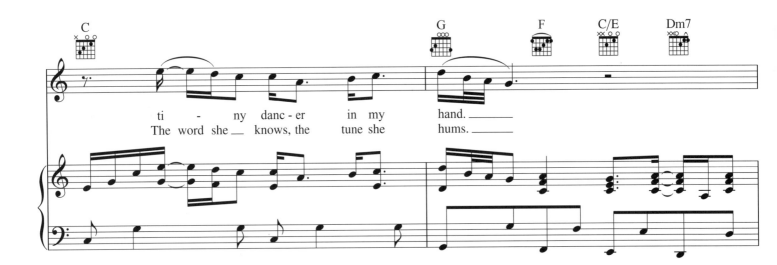

ti - ny danc - er in my hand. _____
The word she _ knows, the tune she hums. _____

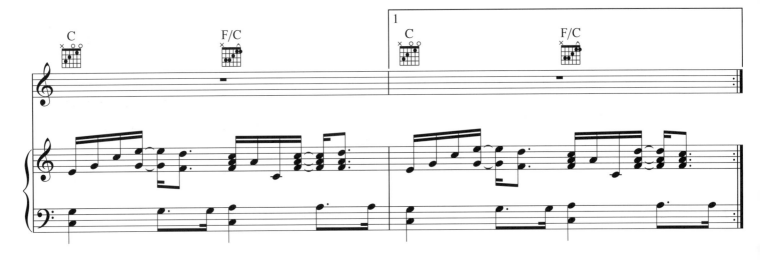

But, oh, how it feels _ so real _

ly - ing here with no one near. __ On - ly you, and you __ can

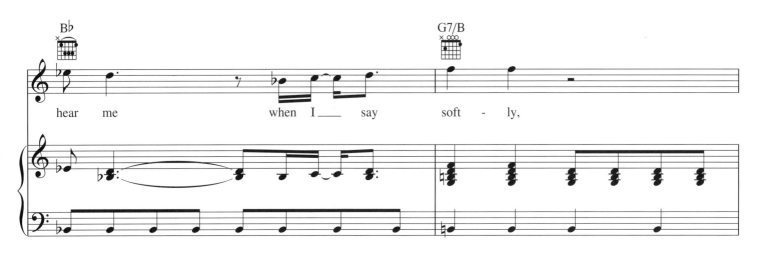

hear me when I __ say soft - ly,

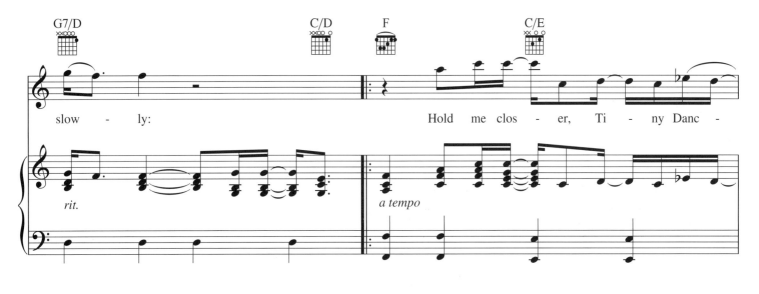

slow - ly: Hold me clos - er, Ti - ny Danc -

rit. *a tempo*

- er. Count the head - lights on __ the high -

way.   Lay me down___ in sheets___ of lin -

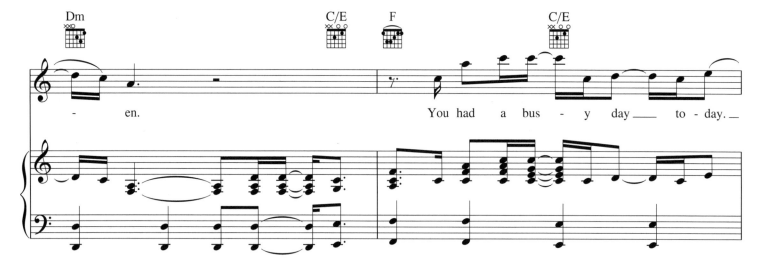

- en.   You had a bus - y day ___ to - day. ___

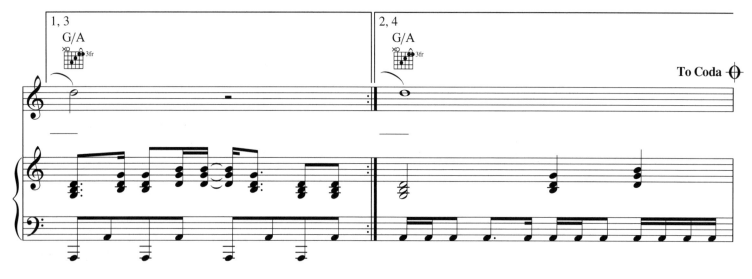

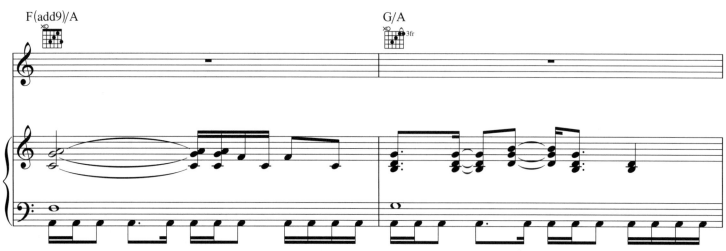

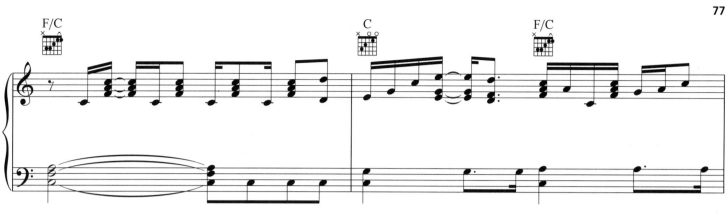

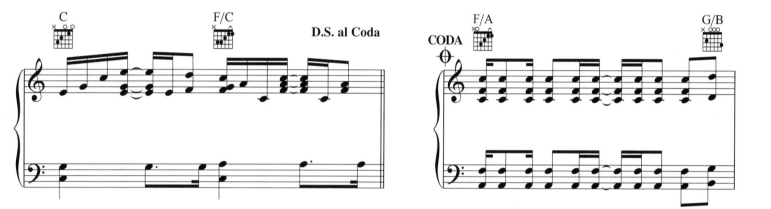

D.S. al Coda

CODA

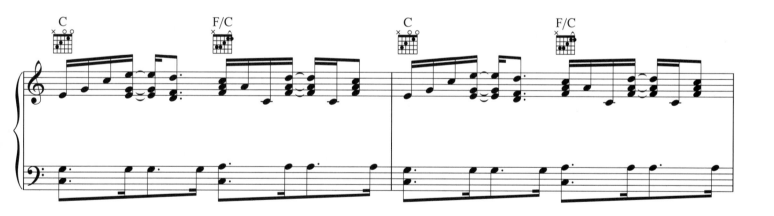

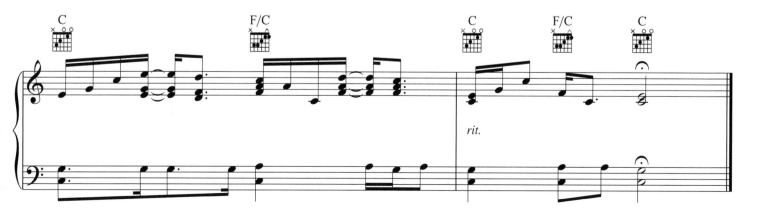

rit.

ROCKET MAN
(I Think It's Gonna Be a Long Long Time)

Words and Music by ELTON JOHN
and BERNIE TAUPIN

Moderately slow, with a beat

She packed _ my bags _ last night pre - flight, ___

Ze - ro hour ___ Nine A. M. ___

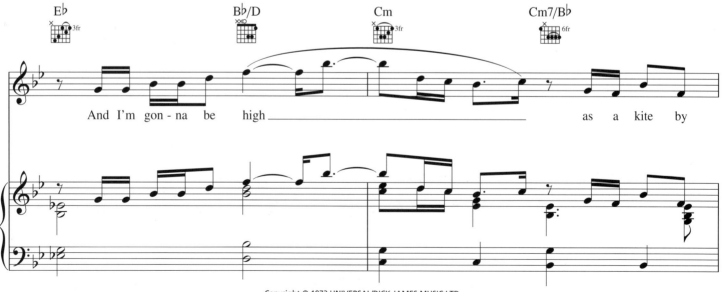

And I'm gon - na be high _____ as a kite by

then.

I miss the earth so much I miss my wife, _____

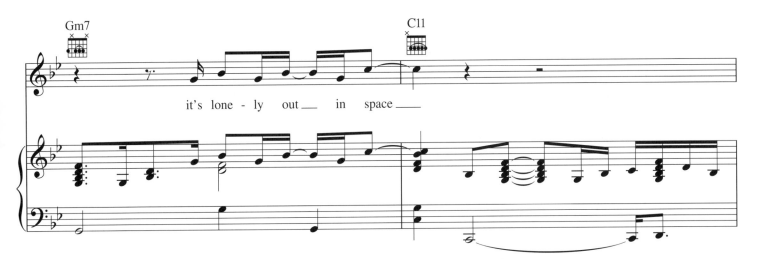

it's lone - ly out __ in space _____

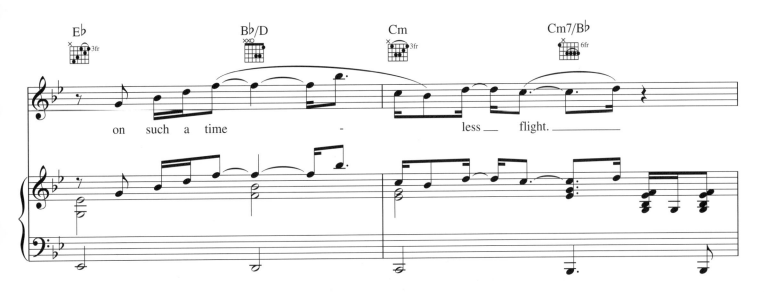

on such a time - less __ flight. _____

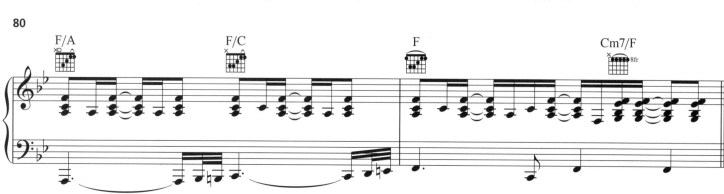

And I think it's gon na be a long _ long time _ till touch - down brings _ me 'round a - gain to find _

_ I'm not the man _ they think I am at home. _ Oh no no no, _ I'm a

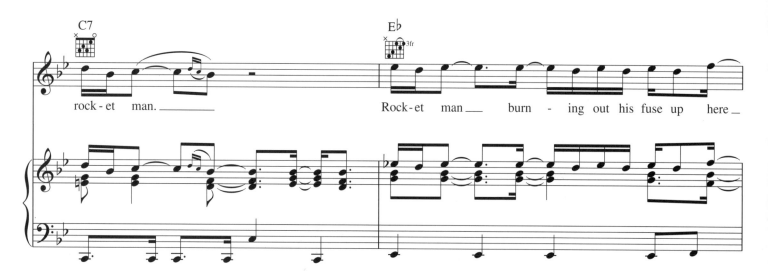

rock - et man. _____ Rock - et man _ burn - ing out his fuse up here _

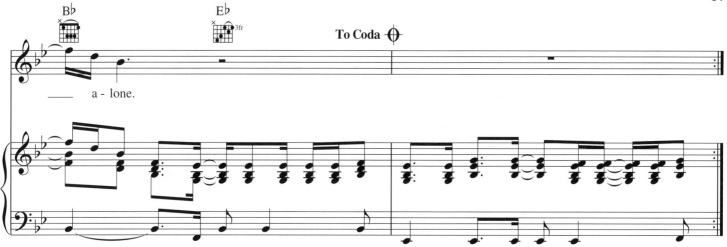

a - lone.

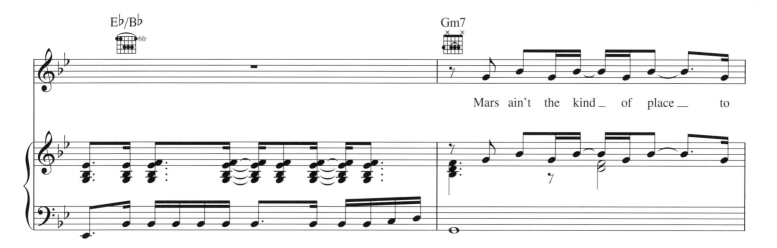

Mars ain't the kind___ of place___ to

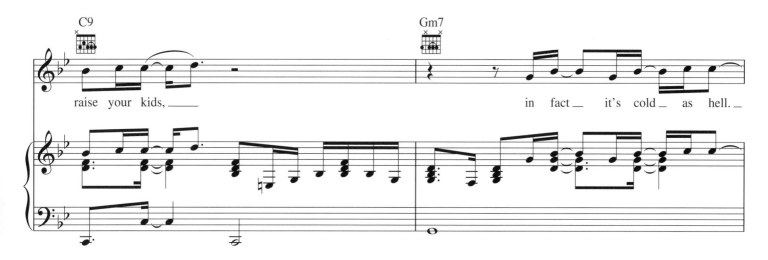

raise your kids,_____ in fact___ it's cold___ as hell.___

And there's no one there___ to___ raise_____

them   if you did.

And all ___ this sci - ence ___   I don't

un - der-stand.   It's just ___ my job ___ five days a week. ___

A rock-et man, _____ a rock-et man. __

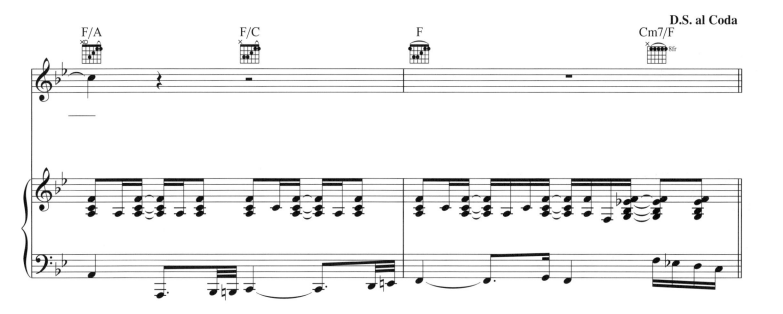

D.S. al Coda

CODA

Repeat and Fade

And I think it's gon-na be a long __ long time. __

SATURDAY NIGHT'S ALRIGHT
(For Fighting)

Words and Music by ELTON JOHN
and BERNIE TAUPIN

With a beat

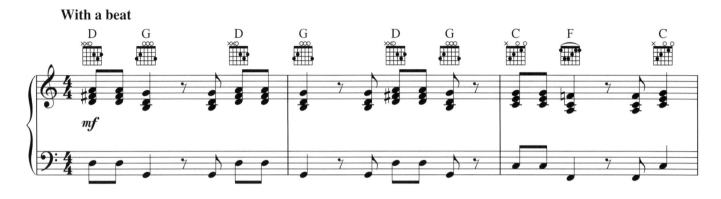

(2nd time) It's get - ting late. __ Have you seen my mates? __ Ma,
packed pret - ty tight in here to - night. __ I'm

tell me when the boys get here. _____ It's sev - en o' - clock __ and I
look - ing for a dol - ly to ____ see me right. I may use a lit - tle mus - cle to

wan-na rock, wan-na get___ a bel-ly full of beer._____ My_
get what I need, I may sink___ a lit-tle drink and shout out she's with me.__ A cou-

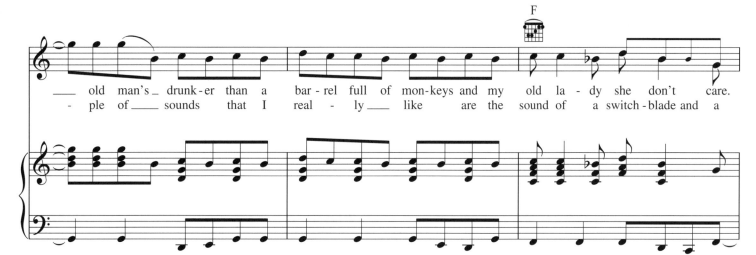

___ old man's_ drunk-er than a bar-rel full of mon-keys and my old la-dy she don't care.
-ple of___ sounds that I real - ly___ like are the sound of a switch - blade and a

mo - tor - bike._ I'm a ju - ve - nile prod-uct of the work - ing class__ whose
My sis - ter looks cute in her brac - es and boots,_ a

hand-ful of grease_ in her hair._____
best friend floats_ in the bot - tom of a glass. Ooh. ____

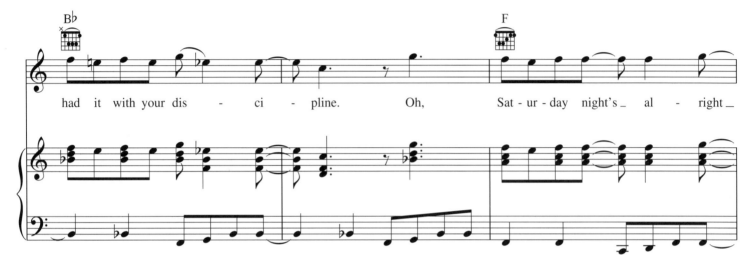

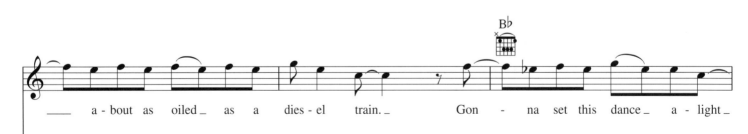

'cause Sat - ur - day night's _ the night _ I like. _ Sat -

- ur - day night's _ al - right _ al - right _ al - right. _

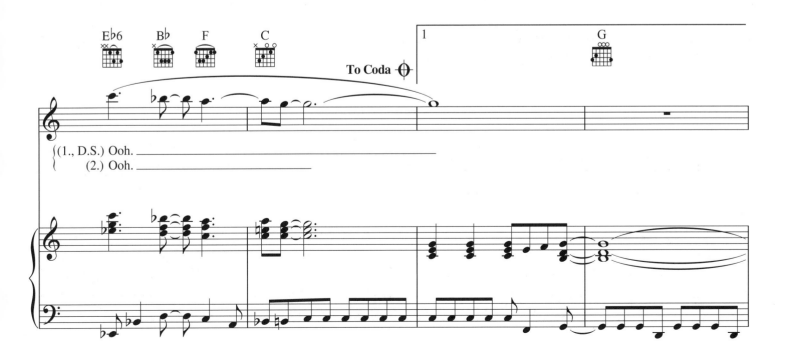

((1., D.S.) Ooh. _
(2.) Ooh. _

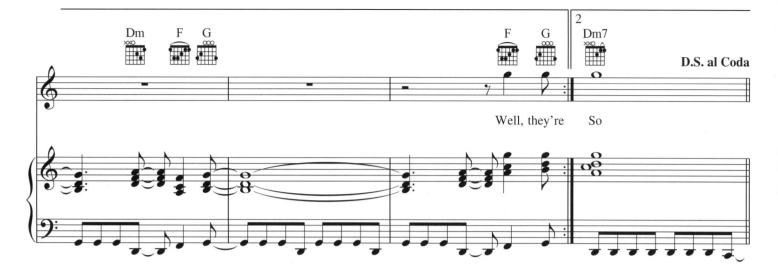

D.S. al Coda

Well, they're   So

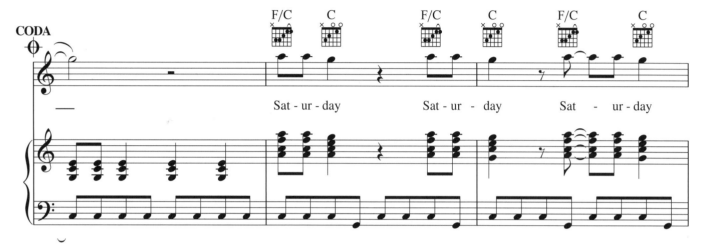

CODA

Sat - ur - day   Sat - ur - day   Sat - ur - day

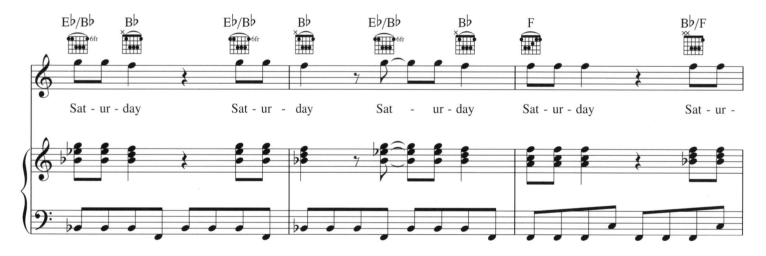

Sat - ur - day   Sat - ur - day   Sat - ur - day   Sat - ur - day   Sat - ur -

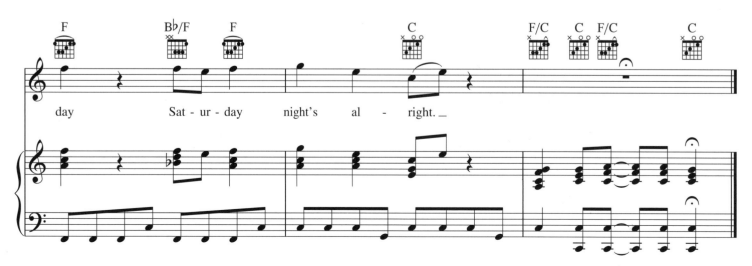

day   Sat - ur - day   night's   al - right. __